Eyes of Distinction

Poems by Tim Pompey

For Jayne and Nancy

Whatever you bury will rise:
bones, secrets, treasures.
The magic of words will find them
and make them sing.
Your choice it is
to find the right tune.

— Dr. Morgan's Southern Idioms, p. 26 —

Published by Tim Pompey

ISBN: 9798439861750

Front Cover Design:
Nancy Delucrezia

tjpompey@gmail.com
timpompey.com

Table of Contents

Eyes of Distinction

I have seen what I have seen.
Don't ask me to backtrack or pretend.
A picture painted cannot be unpainted.
A life lived cannot be unlived.

We are all visions of something.
Look at the world, how it functions.
Are we not the products of many eyes?

I have not come easily to this.
Still, my eyes share what was and is.
Perhaps we clash and rise above it.
Perhaps we simply ignore what's there.

My eyes, your eyes, not the same.
But our sight. That is what we share,
and here, I give you mine.

Let it leaven you and leaven me toward you.
Let it navigate us through muddy currents.
Let it overflow with a plethora of sights—
jostling, colliding, creating life upon life—
till we gather at a great gulf,
many eyes, many visions, many stories.
One human thread that holds us
in its strong, broad hands.

Family Photos @ 1957

All the adults are smiling.
It's what you do in a photo.
I'm all of three and less sure.
My mom and dad are dressed up.
This on a warm California day.
Everyone else is West Coast casual.
It's only a moment in time.
No reason given for the gathering.
55 years later I look back and wonder.
The magic of photography.
The dead resurrected.
The family gathered.
Should I believe this?

What I wish:
The father was real.
The mother was mine.

What a photo cannot tell.
The story itself, the long story.
The story I recall.
After the smiles.
After everyone goes home.
The picture no one captured.

Meanwhile, the sun shines.
Everyone is at their best.
The happiness.
All garnished.

The photo spells it out.
It begs me to believe.
Oh burdened skeptic.
I tell the photo to fuck off.

Mother Issues

The woman in the photograph.
My mother.
Not my mother.
As if I recognize her and yet not.

Yes, we lived together for ten years.
But the day she left town on a bus,
I breathed a sigh of relief.

Not a nice thought to think.
But no regrets either.

I remember feeling unchained
and ready to get on with life.
Year to year,
I dreaded seeing her,
afraid of being recaptured.

Did my friends and family wonder?
Perhaps a moment of suspicion.
He should, they thought.
I shouldn't, I rebuffed.
And so I pantomimed
strictly for appearance sake.

Most people assume
a boy and his mother are sacred.
Not me. Not my mother.

Think of it this way.
When you're stuck in a car
with a perfect stranger,
you're under no obligation.
In this case, the car stopped,
and I jumped out.

She was my mother.
She was not.
I was her son.
I am not.

We were in the same picture.
Just never together.

First Day in Gettysburg

The small boy struggles in the snow.
Behind his mom, he treks to Grandma's house.
Not an "over the river and through the woods" scenario.
It's February and we have just arrived by bus
from California to small-town Gettysburg, SD.

No one has told me why we're here.
I'm eight, old enough to understand.
Yet here we are, bundled up, luggage in hand.

I can't fathom what this world is.
The trip did not include a map.
It's cold as Siberia, but where are we
and why?

Blue sky, white snow.
A boy in limbo.
A mother adrift.

The world has changed.
Without questions or reasons.
As if life itself owes no one,
not my mother, and certainly not me,
a damn bit of explanation
except to say: Keep walking.

Fatherhood

A father I became.
Without plans.

It took years for me to catch up.
I am still reeling.

Holding my breath, a father
I've become.

And now my son a father
to his sons.

Such a long journey start to finish.
Hardly time to say goodbye.

My tendons weaken, but not
the demands.

As if being a father requires acting, lessons,
rehearsal, appearances, critique.

I look in the eyes of my son and see my eyes.
I see us trading roles.

Whatever he feels, about me, about fatherhood
remains undisclosed.

I feel the tendons loosen.
I know that whatever my performance,
he has already moved on.

Greek Imperial Bronze
Circa 27BC – 253AD

This coin I inherited from my father.
I keep it on the wall as a reminder.
No matter the age, we all require money.

My father collected coins.
He valued them more than children.
What wisdom he passed on to me
I could fit on a coin's head.

Imagine who has handled this coin.
What value it brought to someone.
How an empire died
along with its currency.

Today it is wrapped in cardboard
and cellophane, taped to my wall.
An extended journey.

How remarkable the history.
2,200 years.
Me, my father, this Greek Imperial.
Three coins in a pouch
grown obsolete.

Mother and Son

I cannot tell you where we split.
Something in our DNA crashed.
We of flesh and blood
changed bodies, assumed new identities,
lived separately in the same house.

There are assumptions made
about mother and son.
One of them is that we are natural.
But what if the embryo separates?
What if someone else takes up residence?

I can still see you sitting quietly on the couch
gaping into space.
Was that when we flew off?

Perhaps you wondered also
how two people joined at the hip
could be more different than us.

I look at your pictures.
I look at my pictures.
I cannot see the resemblance.
I know who we were.
I simply cannot tell you why.

Lament

Such a wide space between us.
A canyon, a continent, a galaxy.
You would think our movements
would be etched all over us.
Mother's milk. The soft purr of a song.
A dinner. Reading a book.

Explain this shadow across our faces,
neither able to see the other.
Our ebony walls, lightless.

People expect more.
People believe in more.
And for our parts,
we played them till the end.

As if pretense counted for loyalty.

I am confused. Offstage.
After dimming the lights.
What were our lines?
And why the lack of spotlights?

Such a wide space between us.
If I am angry, measure that space.
Stand quietly in the dark.
Feel the solitude.

I am a child of loneliness.
I search for recognition
but my eyes are old.

Even today,
as I throw a thought across this gulf,
I touch nothing.

Snapshots of My Father

The few I have are startling.

The fresh-faced sailor.
The suit and tie family man.
The bearded divorcee.
The bad sweater son.

As if they define chapters
in your self-destruction.

Toward the end,
you repelled your chaos,
as if you had disconnected
from time, family, and empathy.

Your shell haunted our reunions.

You lived in an apartment overwhelmed
by genealogies, coins, and stamps
attached to your life
like barnacles to a boat.

In the end we had to scrape them,
scrub them, toss them
to retrieve your legacy.

A father should offer something
to his children.
I sold the coins and stamps.
I tossed the genealogies.

I have a Greek coin on my wall
and a three-generation picture:
grandfather, father, son.

I miss where you should have been.
I wonder what might have been.

As for what *is* between us:
A fragile string.
A dim view.
A missing cause.

For Grace

If we sat at dinner as we used to,
your reedy body framed by a cigarette
in your bone-thin fingers,
What would you say?

The cards have played out.
The deck is used.
The joker has been claimed.

I suspect as the smoke rings rise,
you would be pleased with yourself.
You warned me after all,
compared me to Sherman,
thought my inclinations suspect.

And you were right.
It turns out we had much in common.
Father, son, the ruinous ghost.

If only I had listened.
If only I had walked a different path.
But alas, you looked at me with iron eyes,
accusatory and wolf-like.

Yes, tonight at dinner,
you would sit and nod
and I would nod with you.

But here's the tricky part.
Seeing what you saw,
walking the walk,
letting the years roll,
would I change anything?

Yes, around that table,
as a young man prepping,
I would take the time,
carefully lean forward,
and offer to shove that cigarette
up your ass.

Then I would smile,
finish my dinner,
and ask politely
if I could be excused.

In Communicado

Full-bodied.
Sound mind.
Accountable.
Reasonable.
In all eyes an adult.

You can't penetrate
the skin, the skull,
the mind, the soul.

So it's left for me to speak
as you stare into my eyes
with that questioning look.

I tell you as forthright as possible.
You can read my birth date
on my driver's license.
The large man with glasses,
the tall one with brown eyes
answers wistfully.

Sometimes a kid.
Sometimes a bigger kid.
Sometimes an adult.
Sometimes all the above
simultaneously.
The tip's tip of the iceberg.
Roiling current
under murky waters.

Stories flow past
chilly depths.
A finger extended.
A mouth open.
Offer me a crack
In your ice and mine.
I will take it.

Hunger

Yes. God sees the sparrow

but this solitary seagull
searching the parking lot
is the view I see
from my window
rush hour
in the drive-thru lane.

The two of us eye each other.

There are no prophets
or parables here.
We aren't sparrows.
Just one man and a gull
on a common mission
in a common parking lot.
Navigate and hunt.

We are hungry.

Oxymorons

Some ironies in my life: I'm good at puzzles.
        I have a knack for shapes.
I took an aptitude test in high school
        and was miserable with hand-eye tests.
I took piano lessons. My sight-reading is marginal.
        Today I play for a living.

Math was my bane. I hit a wall in the 7th grade
        and struggled with algebra.
Today I do the family budget.

I have trouble keeping my thoughts straight
        but I can write like a fiend
and speak in public.
        Sometimes I stutter and struggle socially.
I have human insight. I write poetry.

I am many things to many people, and nothing to many more.
        You might wonder if I am being truthful?
It's a reasonable question.
    I have often wondered the same.

I have come to accept irony and what I don't know.
    I have come to live with awkwardness and what I know.
What baffles me the most in the hem and haw of breathing:
        How to tell the difference?

En Route from Maryland to California

When you're driving two-thousand miles in a small yellow car,
there are hours, days even, when you're neither here nor
elsewhere.

Alone in your vehicle, you watch road signs,
count miles, look at your gas gauge,
keep track of mileage, one town to the next.

The sun comes and goes. The weather changes.
The towns pass. It's all part of a larger landscape.

It doesn't occur to me at that moment that I am homeless.
After all, I'm moving, waiting, thinking about California.
What matters more is where I'm going and why.

Out on the freeway, with huge swaths of open space,
I have time to think, miles to waste, nothing but future.

There are those moments in a small yellow car.
A man sits while the car moves.
A man waits for his destination.
A man forgets about coming and going.
A man meditates about nothing but space.

With only the road. The time it takes to reach someplace.
To get there from other highways.
Then sit and write this poem and still wonder where,
down the road, past lines of demarcation, I am going.

Turnoff I-40 & Highway 325 to Townsend

The turnoff is that final step.
On a sunny day, I clearly see the mountains
framed like a postcard.

I perk up from a long haul across the Cumberland Valley,
Nashville to Sevierville,
and know that I am almost there.

I am not a sentimental Southerner. Not a true hillbilly.
No long family lineage.
No claim to the wars.

What I am is a child of the mountains.
When I first arrived in 1965, they spoke to me.
Wide and blue, hazy and high.

What lived here grew inside me:
Roots, rivers, and rocks.
Bats, fish, and possums.
Heat, trees, and blue skies.

What I drive toward—the mountains.
The luxury of the Smokies.
Yes, I have wandered to California.
But I know home when I see it.

People cannot claim me as their kin.
Some would not claim me at all.
But I wear a t-shirt that says *Tennessee.*

When I turn down that highway,
I am fierce. I am determined. I am focused.
In one slight action, veering one road to the other,
I am a son.

Collage: April 2016

I have a collage photo frame.
Four pictures taken in Tennessee.
Left to right:
A forest. Me in a rocking chair.
A mountain stream. A rustic cabin.

That was a good day.
Sunday. Spring approaching.
Slight chill in the shade.
Trees blossoming.
My high school friend, Jerry.

I told him how much I missed this.
What I couldn't find where I lived.
Jerry grew up here. A photographer.
He deeply sympathized.

I'm sure he wondered:
If you love something, why leave it?
Oh how restless, the heart.
How quick I was to change clothing
and rearrange the furniture.

Parts of me float everywhere
in multiple states.
I am a collage of a collage,
scissors to paper,
shredded and scattered.

I left to escape
and still I am on the lam.
But for a moment,
the man in this picture
is enveloped in his element.

Change the collage in any direction
but leave me in my rocking chair
for one more moment
among the dogwoods and rhododendrons
and the music of the river
on a porch in my breaker and safari hat.

Leave me alone.
I'm happy.

That Perfect Summer

Summer job cooking chicken.
Graduated.
In luscious limbo.
Big man on campus.
These moments.
You can't know them
when they happen.
But there they are.
Me and Mike on a bus.
A day in Knoxville.
A little dough in our pants.
Wake up young man.
You're only here once.
A free day.
A free life.
There and gone.
The moment.
A damn good one.
I had a date
and nothing to lose.
For a breath,
I was the king.

Boys Down at the Creek

Slow moving brown muddy.
Our fishing hole.
Quick check to see if the tree was free.
Then on to other spots.
Fish to catch.
Snakes to bother. Gars.
The fishing was spiritual.
Peeling off bread into dough balls.
Shooting shit. Getting wet.
Looking upriver.
Looking down river.
Imagining the world. Bigger.
Then going home.
In time for dinner.
Who caught what?
Permanent water imprints.
Still not dry.

Daydream Believer

I had a full-blown crush on you—in secret.
I watched and knew I had no chance.
That didn't stop me.

I made up stories. I made it all seem heroic.
I made love to you.
We're talking down and dirty.
The man of the hour skin to skin
without a peep to anyone.

When we graduated, that was that.
I had no choice but to move on.
To other full-blown crushes. Multiple quakes.

When men grow old,
people assume we dissolve from age's battery acid.
Not true. Our minds are dangerous and deep.

There is a hole where you were.
An underground cave. Several caves.
A canyon buried near magma.

The rush still rumbles with cracks and crevices.
Deep in my skull, what remains dark as ebony
is warm to the touch.

If I Had Taken Latin

With the smart kids,
the bright ones with a future.
I always marveled when they got out of class,
how much smarter they were.

I didn't see myself that way.
I was a Spanish student.
Nothing wrong with that.
Millions of people still speak it.
Latin. The dead language.
The smart dead language.

Valedictorians take Latin.
Future doctors and dentists.
Scientists and lawyers.
Pretty girls and likable guys.
The cream of the crop.

I was afraid.
Mrs. McCall with her stern reputation.
Smart kids. Good households.
The future in waiting. Not me.

I went on to earn two graduate degrees.
I learned ancient Greek and Hebrew.
Turns out I had a knack for languages.

Tonight I look back wistfully.
All those folks happy to learn Latin.
I could have sat among them,
been a contender.

I chose different.
I chose safely and did well.
I got straight A's in Spanish.
I was no fool.
I knew where I belonged.

Jenny Adams

I can't understand memories.
Some remain.
Others lose pixelation.
Others disappear entirely.

For instance, that spring evening.
You and I on a bench.
Me, shy as a rabbit,
moving slowly, hopefully.
You, suddenly angry with me.
For reasons still unclear.
The end.

Why does that moment remain?
So many memories like blinking stars.
Some you notice, some you don't.

This random memory sticks.
A pin prick of a hole.
A drop of blood.
A scab.

She remains.
I remain with her.
The heart still longs,
clenches, and lets go.

A memory.
Silent, absent, prescient.
Blink, blink, blink.
It stares at me
while other stars die out.

A Love Poem

In case I forget to mention it,
the good fortune of love
has always been here.

Not that I have appreciated it as I ought
or returned it as I should.
Sometimes the best gifts get piled in a corner.

That is not the case now.
Among our jetsam and flotsam,
I speak with simplicity.

I cannot forget.
You are the giver and the gift.
The one who knows and sees all.

Everyone should be so lucky
to gain what is so rare.
Everyone should be so fortunate
to save the best for last.

The scales have fallen off my eyes.
I am clear-eyed and so are you.

We are two trees woven together.
Intermingled. Inseparable.
Our larger tree grows daily,
leaves green and golden.

Accept my apologies.
Accept my offer.

Remember I was lost and found,
and perhaps, in some small way,
my gratitude will lift you up.

The word or two I offer comes slowly.
Yet even measured in degrees,
it remains the root.

Time Management

What to do with the gift of time?
It was all there in front of me,
but what I made were plans.

Now time is scarce,
but I still have the gift.
At least a small portion.

Plans aside, time only benefits
if you know how to spend it.

Pray tell, you and me,
in our small bungalow,
let us use what we have—

the sliver of sunsets,
the gold and reds,
the flashes of yellow between the clouds,
and consider us rich!

Species

What I was then.
What I am now.
It's hard to recognize either man.
I am built in parts.
Somebody recognizes me.
Somebody doesn't.
It would be nice to be complete.
Like a painting in a museum.
A recognizable, noteworthy attraction
with posters, coffee books, mugs.

What have I become?
Even I am hard pressed to describe it.
The skinny troublemaker.
The hardcore pretender.
The man in the crowd who creates.

You're right. I don't belong.
But I don't *not* belong.
Look at it this way.
As if you're watching a chrysalis.
The incognito side of evolution.
A quiet mutation.
A man. Not a man.
Grown. Invisible.
A new species.

Flight

I have this dream of flying.
Just stretch my arms and rise.

Up to clouds.
Up to sky.
Up to space.

Far past Virgo,
GN-z11,
or anything Milky.

The air will lift me.
Sound will evaporate.

I will ascend and shed heaviness,
be spirit and float freely.

Be a bird.
Be more than a bird.
Be a dream.
Be more than a dream.
And then, with a lapse of consciousness,
in a moment of surrender,
Be nothing at all.

Elder Art

Newsweek suggests people came from many different ancestors,
multiplied in fits and starts, traveled the world,
died out, resurrected, and migrated again.

That is how we, the small band at Westoff Care Center,
came to be here on a warm August night.
Years of morphing, procreation, accidents, persistence.

So mundane, unbiblical, and yet, the brain makes soufflé
from our commonness — life, love, death —
congeals in tiny times and places: restaurants, bedrooms, nursing
homes.

Occasionally it burps out genius. More often, it begets us,
common stiffs, doormats of civilization.

Tonight, as progeny of these old pilgrims, I watch and paint
by words among our elderly, fellow descendants from the African
plains, whose early kin might also, on a long summer night
as they cooked dinner, have imagined the future.

As the same flesh and spirit, I am passing on their DNA,
 a channeler, a revolutionary, a silent arc of unspoken visions
in time and space, to maintain the boil and bubble of evolution,
push toward the shape and thoughts of brains to come,
create the nourishment we need to branch off, stand up straight,

become

human.

Benefits

Take these moments of happiness.
Wrap them tight.
Sit in a restaurant.
Watch a movie.
Assemble a puzzle.
Go for a drive.
Eat a smoothie.
Laugh.

Remember. You only have a limited supply
and no do-overs.
A point in time.
A moment flashes.
This is us. Smiling.
Gone.

Quietly burnish them to a high polish.
Estate planning 101.
A bird in the hand.
A lovely songbird.

Take another moment if you can.
Take two, even.
Relish the chance to be generous.

Chasing Beauty

There is always the wall
changing heights
and thickness,
and me scaling
the word
the note
the line
bouncing
like an echo.

Beyond it, beauty,
the ache of it,
limbs reaching
both ways.

But the wall
and people's eyes
perceiving
and me wondering:
Is this my imagination?

Staring at the Sky

On a day like today
I can lay on my back,
stare into the Celtic blue,
and imagine there's something else
or someone else staring back.

The sun illuminates
yet never reveals.
The sky stretches,
a solid sheet.

I have not given up belief.
Not in the sky nor the sun.
What I fail to see
is what's beyond.

Different speakers speak
and swear their allegiance.
The immutable sky sees all of us.

Today, for instance.
Beauty so fresh I can taste it,
I just gaze up and wish
I could swim here,
eyes open, absorbed until
there is neither me nor blue.
Neither here nor there.
Neither up nor down.
Only presence.
Only. You.

The Book of Life

The story is almost complete.
Now I understand.
The subtleties. The nuance.
The mistakes. The recoveries.
I took the long route.
Old age, the last chapter.
Now that I have walked through it,
all that remains—the ending.

I'm staring back
as if to make sense of this.
The question begs me,
burns a hole in my pocket:
In God's pure omnipotence,
was the real writing
ever mine to start with?

Ten Random Thoughts

I.

People keep reminding me.
God is in charge.
By way of random loop thinking.
Call it either wishful or negligent.

God's thoughts are quiet.
Humans are more boisterous.

I can't tell who runs the asylum.
I'm willing to bet.
It isn't me.

II.

What does it take to murder someone?
Training.
Hate.
Ruthlessness.
Also weapons.
The product of our ingenuity.
In the right hands
they are as moral as bird eggs.

III.

You wake up and discover
you've been brainwashed.
Just wake up

like you're in a bad dream.
I can't explain it.
Not the waking up.
The sleeping part.
I had my eyes open.
What I saw.
The nightmare of it.
I woke up and can't remember
a damn thing.

IV.

What is love?
It's pasted all over the news.
In print.
In books.

There's no lack of information.
But I can't find it.
Anywhere.

You'd think
as high tech as I am
I could find a map
or a picture.

Man in love.
Women in love.
Child in love.

It's like being pinned to the ground
with no trace of gravity.

I'm in love.
That much is obvious.
So why am I staring
at a blank picture?

V.

I've watched the moon.
It has no cheese.
None.
Ask me how I know?
I can't tell you.
Call it faith.
If you don't believe me
look for yourself.
Bring a sharp knife.
Try cutting a slice.
Keep trying.
Sooner or later
you'll figure it out.

VI.

There is a concerted push
to make me patriotic.
I feel a hand on my shoulder.
Hot breath in my ear.
There was a time
I might have listened.

Maybe today the knife in my back
is a little too sharp.

VII.

One good turn deserves another.
I suppose that's assumed.
Depending on where
and how well you turn.
I suppose it assumes
the turn is good.
Not everyone sees a turn
as welcome.
I have turned quite a bit
in my life.
I thought I was okay.
What a surprise
when I saw the turn cut.
I don't like the sight of blood.
I've decided in my life
to simply stop turning.

VIII.

We make pictures
of each other.
Form opinions.
Photographically.
Rapidly.
Instantaneously.
Click. Click.
You ask.
What's wrong with this picture?
Check your camera.
Perhaps your resolution
is too limited.

IX.

I asked my wife
for forgiveness.
She asked me
to be considerate.
I'm learning
to ask less.
To be careful
what I ask for.
Some choices are hard.
I wasn't built in a day.
The road to Rome
is crooked.
My wife knows that
and still asks.

X.

And finally.
You get what you pay for.
Sometimes you get what you don't pay for.
If I knew the difference
I would be a very rich man.

Deliverance and Redemption

I prayed to God for deliverance.
From sex.
From loneliness.
From my own family.

I thought miracles were attainable,
that prayer gave me a leg up
and wrenched heaven wide open.
After all. I spoke in tongues.

We shouted. Raised the roof. Danced in the aisle.
There were moments I thought
I could be like Jesus.

But I wasn't. Changed.
God hadn't changed.
Nothing had changed.
Exhausted, I would fall asleep.

Things worked out as they worked out.
No deliverance, but a life, nonetheless.
I'm lucky to be alive.

And yet the great gulf.
The slough of spoken words.
The lack of drama.
Hearing of Jesus' life,
those moments when I hungrily sought
stories so distant.

Truly, the man I believed in was not me.
The man I am was not the man who prayed.
The deliverance I craved did not arrive.
The tongues I spoke did not translate.

The will of God is still a mystery.
As if I meant to poke through a black veil
with a sharp stick.
One good thrust should have worked.

The veil. Tough as Teflon.
The silence. Still.

Confession and Forgiveness

I seek forgiveness.

If only I could backtrack
and reimagine myself,
but those cords are cut.

From a window,
I have a clear view out.
Those far beyond
can't see or hear me.
They have long passed
out of sight.

I am unseen,
perhaps unwelcome.
Surely unknown.
Yet I have not forgotten
the man blunt and careless
and God keeps good records.

It will come soon enough.
Mercy. Judgment. Revelation.
A whole book jarred and shaken.

I seek forgiveness.
Will forgiveness seek me?
Does regret even matter
for these distant scars?
The blood stains dry and cold.

Elegy for a Lassen Meadow

Oh grass and trees,
water and light.
If only I were this lovely.
If only I stayed in one place.
A canopy for song birds.
What I might give and receive.

Alas. I cannot be anything but me.
The man gazing. The despoiler.
The polluter. Family to disruptors.
Shovelers. Diggers. Trackers.
Apologies for my nature.

I am grateful for this view.
This multi-colored canvas.
This one day of esprit de corps.
I am sorry for my footprint.

Soon enough, I will dissolve to soil.
Ashes scattered in the air.
Nutrients for your roots.
I am anxious for the day.
To be friends with the wind.
To be tickled by grass.
To be blanketed by snow.

Sitting as I am for one blissful moment,
I can only hope it will be here.

Big Country

The swing between heaven and hell rests on a tightrope.
Make the wrong decision, die awkwardly,
and the suffering is immense.

The sword still hangs over my head.
Some folks wonder.
God must wonder.
Every Sunday, I wonder.

In my imagination, I picture the afterlife
as a big country where my feet will naturally walk
in the right direction.

Beyond, something in the light and the land,
as if a great architect planned it.

Of course, I could be wrong.
The threat may be real,
and the suffering.

What would convince me otherwise?
Perhaps the existence of beauty,
something in the soul that feeds on it
as essential nourishment.

The hue I catch. The sound I hear.
The stir I feel.

At great risk, I am willing to forsake the tightrope,
and let whatever lies beyond woo me.
It is not for nothing that I swing toward it,
this flourish of color and glimmering elegance,
the pull and push of creation.

In the beginning, as if the call is still there.
As if its origin is born in me, and as its sire,
I gracefully move home.